#BESTBITCH

best
bitch

BEST BITCH

Summersdale Publishers Ltd
46 West Street
Chichester
West Sussex
PO19 1RP
UK

www.summersdale.com

Printed and bound in the Czech Republic

ISBN: 978-1-84953-912-8

Substantial discounts on bulk quantities of Summersdale books are available to corporations, professional associations and other organisations. For details contact Nicky Douglas by telephone: +44 (0) 1243 756902, fax: +44 (0) 1243 786300 or email: nicky@summersdale.com.

best
bitch

summersdale

To.......Bella Donna.......

From.......Lauri.......

True friends are like diamonds – bright, beautiful, valuable and always in style.

Nicole Richie

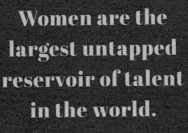

Women are the
largest untapped
reservoir of talent
in the world.

Hillary Clinton

**Some girls are
just born with glitter
in their veins**

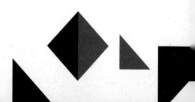

NO ONE CAN MAKE YOU FEEL INFERIOR WITHOUT YOUR CONSENT.

Eleanor Roosevelt

If a woman is sufficiently ambitious, determined and gifted – there is practically nothing she can't do.

Helen Lawrenson

Never give up, for
that is just the place
and time that the
tide will turn.

Harriet Beecher Stowe

BITCH #1
BITCH #2

= BEST FRIEND
GOALS

I like you because we hate the same stuff

ONE IS NOT BORN, BUT RATHER BECOMES, A WOMAN.

Simone de Beauvoir

You only live once,
but if you do it right,
once is enough.

Mae West

#Bae

You grow up the day you have the first real laugh at yourself.

Ethel Barrymore

A LOT OF PEOPLE ARE AFRAID TO SAY WHAT THEY WANT. THAT'S WHY THEY DON'T GET WHAT THEY WANT.

Madonna

SHE'S BRIGHT LIKE GLITTER AND BUBBLY LIKE CHAMPAGNE...

**AND SHARP
LIKE BARBED
WIRE**

**Wherever we are,
it is our friends that
make our world.**

· Henry Drummond

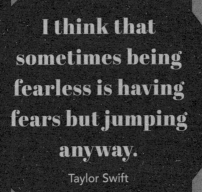

I think that sometimes being fearless is having fears but jumping anyway.

Taylor Swift

PRINCESS?

NO BITCH, YOU'RE A QUEEN

**Everything in my life,
every answer in my life,
every opportunity is
always my decision.**

Nicki Minaj

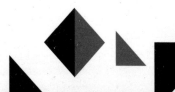

IN MY MOMENTS OF DOUBT I'VE TOLD MYSELF FIRMLY –
IF NOT ME, WHO? IF NOT NOW, WHEN?

Emma Watson

You have what it takes
to be a victorious,
independent,
fearless woman.

Tyra Banks

We're not afraid
to sparkle

Nothing is better than a friend, unless it is a friend with chocolate.

Linda Grayson

BITCH SQUAD

There is nothing like puking
with somebody to make
you into old friends.

Sylvia Plath

When a woman
becomes her own
best friend life
is easier.

Diane von Fürstenberg

She's fleeky

A FRIEND TO ALL IS A FRIEND TO NONE.

Aristotle

I HOPE WE'RE FRIENDS UNTIL WE DIE...

**THEN I
HOPE WE
STAY GHOST
FRIENDS
AND WALK
THROUGH
WALLS
SCARING THE
SHIT OUT OF
PEOPLE**

A true friend is someone who lets you have total freedom to be yourself.

Jim Morrison

You can't do it alone... Other people and other people's ideas are often better than your own.

Amy Poehler

1 UNIVERSE
7 SEAS
9 PLANETS
204 COUNTRIES
809 ISLANDS

AND I HAD THE PRIVILEGE OF MEETING YOU

I embrace mistakes. They make you who you are.

Beyoncé

BITCHES GET STUFF DONE.

Tina Fey

I'm not interested
in money, I just want
to be wonderful.

Marilyn Monroe

You are
fierce

Be strong, love and believe in yourself.

Emma Watson

DON'T GET BITTER, JUST GET BETTER.

Alyssa Edwards

GURL

GANG

If you obey all the
rules, you miss
all the fun.

Katharine Hepburn

A woman is like a teabag – you can't tell how strong she is until she gets into hot water.

Anonymous

Ignore the haters

THE MOST COURAGEOUS ACT IS STILL TO THINK FOR YOURSELF. ALOUD.

Coco Chanel

**Life's too short
to bullshit.**

Naomi Campbell

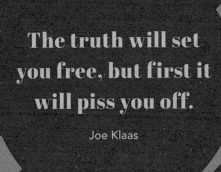

The truth will set you free, but first it will piss you off.

Joe Klaas

My baddest bitch

THE MOST
BEAUTIFUL
DISCOVERY
TRUE FRIENDS
MAKE IS THAT
THEY CAN GROW
SEPARATELY
WITHOUT
GROWING APART.

Elisabeth Foley

YOU ONLY LIVE ONCE,

SO YOU MIGHT AS WELL BE A BADASS

Chin up –
we've got this

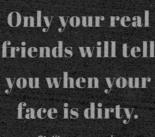

Only your real
friends will tell
you when your
face is dirty.

Sicilian proverb

BEST FUCKING
FRIENDS

I DON'T WANT
OTHER PEOPLE
TO DECIDE WHO
I AM. I WANT TO
**DECIDE THAT
FOR MYSELF.**

Emma Watson

The important thing is not what they think of me, but what I think of them.

Queen Victoria

Keep your friends close. Buy your enemies something cool.

Lena Dunham

YOU'RE MY FAVOURITE BITCH

**TO BITCH
ABOUT
BITCHES WITH**

I think women are foolish to pretend they are equal to men, they are far superior and always have been.

William Golding

**OWN WHO
YOU ARE**

It's easier to be brave when you're not alone.

Amy Poehler

No one has ever
been able to tell me
I couldn't do something
because I was a girl.

Anne Hathaway

Soul sister

'WHY THE
FUCK NOT ME?'
SHOULD BE
YOUR MOTTO.

Mindy Kaling

No one will ever
be as entertained
by us as us

Doubt is a killer. You just have to know who you are and what you stand for.

Jennifer Lopez

Say yes, and you'll figure it out afterwards.

Tina Fey

TRUE FRIENDSHIP COMES WHEN SILENCE BETWEEN TWO PEOPLE IS COMFORTABLE.

David Tyson Gentry

**OUR LAUGHS?
LIMITLESS**

**OUR
MEMORIES?
COUNTLESS**

OUR
FRIENDSHIP?
FUCKING
FANTASTIC

A friend is someone who understands your past, believes in your future, and accepts you just the way you are.

Anonymous

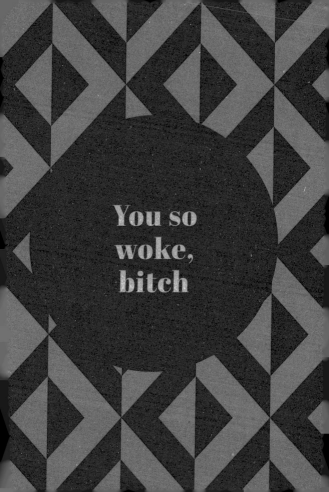

You so
woke,
bitch

**WE R 2 FAB
4 YOU**

DON'T BE LIKE ANYONE ELSE.

FIND YOUR VOICE, YOUR SCRIPT, YOUR RHYTHMS.

Jill Soloway

It's the friends you can call up at 4 a.m. that matter.

Marlene Dietrich

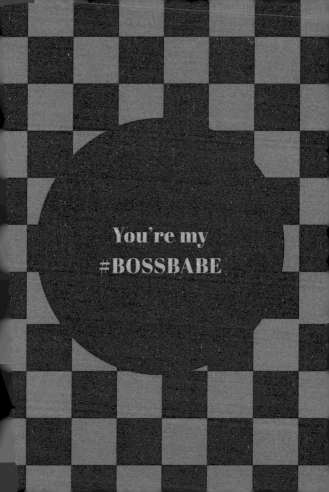

You're my
#BOSSBABE

It is not so much our
friends' help that helps
us as the confident
knowledge that
they will help us.

Epicurus

TOO GLAM
TO GIVE
A DAMN

A friend is one
that knows you as
you are, accepts
what you have
become and allows
you to grow.

Anonymous

Always be a
first-rate version
of yourself, instead
of a second-rate
version of
somebody else.

Judy Garland

I THOUGHT
I WAS
NORMAL...

**UNTIL I MET
MY BEST
FRIEND**

If you think you're too small to have an impact, try going to bed with a mosquito.

Anita Roddick

SASSY
SINCE
BIRTH

I don't care what is written about me so long as it isn't true.

Dorothy Parker

**Never dull your
shine for
somebody
else.**

Tyra Banks

BOYS ARE WHATEVER,

**BEST FRIENDS
ARE FOREVER**

You can't be afraid of what people are going to say, because you're never going to make everyone happy.

Selena Gomez

I SAY IF I'M
BEAUTIFUL. I SAY
IF I'M STRONG.
YOU WILL NOT
DETERMINE MY
STORY – I WILL.

Amy Schumer

SHE BELIEVED
SHE COULD

SO SHE DID

**Girls should
never be afraid
to be smart.**

Emma Watson

Your vibe attracts
your tribe

Life's a bitch. You've got to go out and kick ass.

Maya Angelou

THINK LIKE A
QUEEN. A QUEEN
IS NOT AFRAID
TO FAIL.
FAILURE IS
ANOTHER
STEPPING STONE
TO GREATNESS.

Oprah Winfrey

DEAR BESTIE,

I HONESTLY DON'T KNOW WHAT I'D DO WITHOUT YOU

I'm tough, ambitious, and I know exactly what I want. If that makes me a bitch, OK.

Madonna

**My dear fellow,
who will let you?
The point is,
who will stop me?**

Ayn Rand

BEST FRIEND IS A PROMISE

NOT A LABEL

Bitches for life

THE THING
WOMEN HAVE
YET TO LEARN IS
NOBODY GIVES
YOU POWER.
YOU JUST
TAKE IT.

Roseanne Barr

#GIRLPOWER

I am not afraid;
I was born to
do this.

Joan of Arc

I figure, if a girl wants to be a legend, she should just go ahead and be one.

Calamity Jane

ABOVE ALL, BE THE HEROINE OF YOUR LIFE, NOT THE VICTIM.

Nora Ephron

WE'LL ALWAYS BE BEST FRIENDS

BECAUSE YOU KNOW TOO MUCH

Nothing can dim the light which shines from within.

Maya Angelou

#LIKEABOSS

Women have been trained to speak softly and carry a lipstick. Those days are over.

Bella Abzug

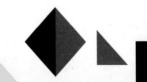

FEMALE FRIENDSHIPS THAT WORK ARE RELATIONSHIPS IN WHICH WOMEN HELP EACH OTHER BELONG TO THEMSELVES.

Louise Bernikow

OMG same

A best friend is like a four leaf clover, hard to find, and lucky to have.

Sarah Jessica Parker

KEEP CALM

**AND LOVE
YOUR BFF**

True friends are those who really know you but love you anyway.

Edna Buchanan

THE BEST MIRROR IS A FRIEND'S EYE.

Gaelic proverb

SURROUND YOURSELF WITH THE THINGS YOU LOVE...

DISCARD
THE REST

I'm a big believer
in accepting yourself
the way you are and
not really worrying
about it.

Jennifer Lawrence

I think about my best friendship... as like a great romance of my young life.

Lena Dunham

GROW OLD GRACEFULLY? NO CHANCE.

WE'LL BE TEARING UP THE NURSING HOME TOGETHER

I only roll with goddesses

DON'T BE AFRAID TO SPEAK UP FOR YOURSELF. KEEP FIGHTING FOR YOUR DREAMS!

Gabby Douglas

**A girl should be
two things: who and
what she wants.**

Coco Chanel

Attitude is everything.

Diane von Fürstenberg

RESTING

BITCH FACE

Don't waste your energy trying to educate or change opinions... Do your thing and don't care if they like it.

Tina Fey

Partners
in crime

You're only young
once, but you can be
immature forever.

Germaine Greer

ANY DAY SPENT WITH YOU IS MY FAVOURITE DAY. SO TODAY IS MY NEW FAVOURITE DAY.

A. A. Milne

We put the hate
in 'whatever'

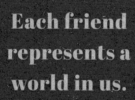

Each friend
represents a
world in us.

Anaïs Nin

True friendship resists time, distance and silence.

Isabel Allende

FAMILY FIRST.
WORK SECOND.
REVENGE THIRD.

Lena Dunham

If you haven't learned the meaning of friendship, you really haven't learned anything.

Muhammad Ali

Other women
who are killing it
should motivate you,
thrill you, challenge
you and inspire you.

Taylor Swift

HOLY SHIT BITCH –

YOU'RE THE BEST

Sometimes you just have to put on lip gloss and pretend to be psyched.

Mindy Kaling

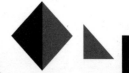

#SQUADGOALS

There's power in looking silly and not caring that you do.

Amy Poehler